I
entered
without
words

PRINCETON SERIES OF CONTEMPORARY POETS
Susan Stewart, series editor

For other titles in the Princeton Series of Contemporary Poets see the end of this volume.

I entered without words

poems

jody gladding

PRINCETON UNIVERSITY PRESS
Princeton and Oxford

Published by Princeton University Press
41 William Street, Princeton, New Jersey 08540
6 Oxford Street, Woodstock, Oxfordshire OX20 1TR

press.princeton.edu

Library of Congress Cataloging-in-Publication Data

Names: Gladding, Jody, 1955– author.
Title: I entered without words : poems / Jody Gladding.
Description: Princeton : Princeton University Press, 2022. | Series: Princeton series of
    contemporary poets | Text in English, with some poems translated into French on facing pages.
Identifiers: LCCN 2021053680 (print) | LCCN 2021053681 (ebook) | ISBN 9780691238951
    (hardback) | ISBN 9780691238968 (paperback) | ISBN 9780691238975 (ebook)
Subjects: BISAC: POETRY / General | POETRY / Women Authors | LCGFT:
    Experimental poetry.
Classification: LCC PS3557.L2914 I15 2022 (print) | LCC PS3557.L2914
    (ebook) | DDC 811/.54—dc23/eng/20220124
LC record available at https://lccn.loc.gov/2021053680
LC ebook record available at https://lccn.loc.gov/2021053681

British Library Cataloging-in-Publication Data is available

Editorial: Anne Savarese and James Collier
Production Editorial: Ellen Foos
Text and Jacket/Cover Design: Pamela L. Schnitter
Production: Erin Suydam
Publicity: Jodi Price and Carmen Jimenez
Copyeditor: Jodi Beder

Jacket/Cover Credit: Nene Humphrey, *Ménerbes 91909*, ink, pastel on paper.

This book has been composed in Adobe Garamond and Scala Sans

Printed on acid-free paper. ∞

Printed in the United States of America

10 9 8 7 6 5 4 3 2 1

Contents

Note to Readers

For these poems, through-lines in bold offer a way in. Other words constellate around the through-lines, and readers are free to move about the page as they please—there is no right or wrong way to proceed. The poem opens into a three-dimensional space where things can happen simultaneously. And differently with each reading. For some poems, there are both English and French versions. These appear together as facing pages.

I

entered

without

words

I   entered

without   words

for

purple

the   mother   aster

tongue

yellow

deep   summer   center

licked

star

me

into

articulate

being

that

taut   serenity

of

water

a   **mare**

can   ripple

I   have   never   been

calm

only   hugged

the   smooth   flesh

of

her   neck

sometimes

ready

to   fly

this

appeared

to   be

quietude

la sérénité crispée

de

l'eau

la jument

se fait frissonner

je n'étais jamais

calme

j'ai serré

quelquefois

la chair lisse

de

son encolure

prête à voler

ça

ressemblait à

la quiétude

3

at my

approach

a shrill

call

now

a green branch

silent

rearranged
r   d

shaking

that

bird

becomes

a show

listen

of

composes

feathers

itself

either

have   **I**

been   a

                                                    redpoll

                                                              flock

                            out

                        early

            or   late

                    attended

        particularly

                            to

                                the

sharp-shinned

                        hawk

                                            scattering

                            birds

au soir

la crête de **la montagne**

engloutit

le reste

du soleil

les hirondelles

reflètent

sa lumière

tournent

autour

des murs de **la** ville

à la recherche

des **blessure**s

ouvertes

toward   nightfall

        the   mountain

               swallows

                        the   last

flashing   of the sun

back

       its   **light**

    circl**in**g

                the city walls

in search of

     the   **open**

              wounds

what

        my

        kind

neighbor

        asks

of

        me

a **quest**ion

        along

ticks

        this

path

we share

with

deer

leaves   dripping

after   rain

I

like

out   here

my   thoughts

thin   clouds

having

late

crickets

nothing

puffballs

on moss

to   do

with

me

guest

awakened at night   *b*olt upright

in wind

a l*e*af

settles back into leaf mol*d*

on   this   green

                                                            our

                                                                    live

                                                                            stock

                                                    exchange

                                                                of   **languages**

the   commons-

                                                        shares

        wealth

                                                                    no   one   owns

            place

                    wherein   so much

                                                        give

                                                        and

                                                                take

                                                        our

                                                words-

                                    graze

11

another

morning

in   the river

valley

waking early

so much

to do

he*a*vy

li*f*ting

w*o*nderin*g*

why

does

it

fall

to

me

but

I

could

still   believe

in

the

dark   night

work

shifts

while   tides

you

of

idleness

washing

have

up

something

light!   worth

house

keeping

13

why not

                                               handpick

           call

                                   the

                                                 goose

                                            berry

         it

                               rose

  all

                               chafer

             harvest

                                               leaves

                                        skeletonized

that can be gleaned

                       ground

                           flat

                                   beneath

                             my thumb

in

this

        my black

            currants

heart

                full   to   bursting

        stung by

    a   hornet

of   summer

gleams

                my child

lightning   storms

        never far

            off

whose

playground

is   th**is**

the   fig   tree

the   stinging   nettle

swings

yes

little   **girl**

in   bright   colors

I'll   **push**   you

not   **so**   *high !*

higher *!*

à **qui est**

cette aire

de jeu

le figuier

l'ortie brû**la**nte

les balançoires

oui

petite **fille**

aux couleurs vives

que

je peux te **pousse**r

pas **si** *haut !*

plus **haut** *!*

messy

br**ea**kfast

                                    I chew *t*hrough th**e** co*r*d

        devour the sac

these

small

bells in many

our young

herds

tatooed

registers

rippling

our **damage**

infirms

radiantly

their

flesh

hors des gonds

un volet bat

je quitte

la maison

d'es fen**être**s

en plein vent

secouée

les feuilles

du chêne vert

frottées

du ciel

unhinged

shutter banging

I left

the house

to

windows

shaken

through

leaves

blasted

scrub   oak

sky   clean

I lay

amazed at

in   how

    my

                                                          all

        sickness

                                                              that could be

                                        the   **sky**

    bed

                                                                        firmament

                                            blue

                        flax   **kept**

linen   thread

                                                        spinning

the

migrations

monarch

thin

what

vanishing

it

means

point **to**

stragglers

when

be

refugees

habitat

reduced

flook

to

deserts

safety

grow

strength

smaller

in

numbers

why

keeping

an   arroyo   this   wild

space

my   hand

open

is

a   promise

not

empty

does

matter

to

hold

rain

all   suspect   clothing   must   be   burned
                        a   single

the   poor
                                        leather
                                                            epidemic

hide
                        jacket
                                                passed
                                                                        from   one
                                                                                    to
                                                                                        another

                                                        what
            for   warmth

                                                        they
                                                                        gather
                                                                        around

                                a
                                                                    lit
                trash
                                            can

                                        fire

who

is that

a barred owl

call

cooks for

mid-day

cooks

you

a scrap of meat

for

saying

taxol

dripping

thank

into

you

pellet of fur

a vein

and bone

thank you

a

to the chemo nurse

w

who brings

w

a **w**arm

l

l

b**l**anket

this

tortoise shell

suggests

capsized

how

ribs

to   turn

were

back   to

the

first

shelter

rafters

sky

thousands of years

before

was

your

hand

I too

rough

opens

over

my scar

abraded

basalt

to

a petroglyph

wave

dark

who will speak

for us

cold

Blind   of earth

Willie   Johnson

was

the

ground

song

humming and moaning

ranges

beyond

night

our

solar system

in

the

winter

stone

chapel

white

monks

pressed

tongue

against

the

vaulted

roof

of

the

mouth

singing

dans

la chapelle

les moines

d'hiver

blancs

se pressent

la langue

contre

la voûte

en pierre

palatine

chantant

that

simple

lightning

out

of

les ténèbres

un éclat

complicated

darkness

de tonnerre

may

the sound

rise

of

thunder

one hand

clapping*!*

taking

over

we   rode

corners

your   **cities**

bikes

storm

too

drains

fast

the

serrated

cindor   **grasses**

blocks

will

growing

up

through

asphalt

skinned

our

knees

( )

an empty room

an artist's

best friend

does

not always

is

how

allow

time

fail

ure

for

pleas

boredom

differ

the artist

on any

given

morning

I might have said

to

sway

enter

this

art

they

honed

of

sidling up

to

their

muses & angels

rusted

knives

silence

voilà

                        les   poetes

                                       qui

                              aiguisent

l'art

                de   s'app**roche**r

                de

                  biais

                                    leurs

                                couteaux

des

          muses **et ange**s

                            roulllés

ce qui

affleure

merci

pour

ce sont

les ~~couches~~

très   belles

"ratures"

profondeurs

votre

~~lettre~~ écriture

des

ruines

what

surfaces

thank you

for

are

your

~~sedimentation~~

very beautiful

thinking

"cross-outs"

depths

~~strata~~

to write

of

ruins

41

why everything beautiful

sunlight t*h*rough   *u*ndergrowth

morning mis*t*   ri*s*ing

in

that cut

pourquoi

toutes les belles choses

la lumière du matin

à travers
la *pi*nède

la brume

*qu*i

s'élève
dans cette **ent**aille

lost

in

all

the   skyline

glass and steel

little   facades

screens

I love

the readers
brick

buildings

with

their

fire

books
escapes

look back

        at me   Eurydice

                                  steadies her phone

                         my love   to take

                                       the picture

          I   can't

                              be

                                      the

says Orpheus

                             old

                           long

     as he

                             story

              turns

                       goes

                here

                              a

                              n$_{ot}$

                                h$_{er}$

                          way

last

to *g*ive myself   to   wind

                                over

                                                                        water

                now
what

                                                        t**o**

                                        call

                                    thi**s**

            way

        hom**e**

dernière

m'abandonner   au   vent

                              au-dessus

                                                              de   l'eau

                                                        maintenant

              comment

          s'appelle

                                                  chez

                                                  nous

                    cette

          v*oie*

with

winter

came

foreclosure

a **deficiency** of

cold

hollows

and

still

we   would   take

sheltered

places

in

snow

banks

this   news   it turns

                from

                              out

                                                                              thin   air

                                         of

                                                                                                          sharply

                                              so   **no**w

                                                            you're leaving

                                         where

                                                            here   colder

                    me

looking   up

                                                       snow

                    into

                                                                 sparks

                         the inflnite

                                                       white

49

paper

*w*inter

stretc*h*es

long

th*i*n

s*t*ems

stars

op*e*n

a

these

stiff   winter grasses

how

the

arcs   they*ir*   *angled shadows*

wind

makes

them

bend

to   the   task

which

in   is

more

snow

beautiful *?*

51

la mort

n'a pas

arasé

comme

le lichen

je grimpe à

la montagne

l'espérance

blanche

de

la

neige

death

has not

eroded

like   lichen

I've clambered up

the **hope**fulness

a   mountain

of

snow

I   seek

the   ice

cold

shock

and

solitary

motive

of

a

mountain

from

which

I

spring

à la

montagne

aiguë

et

solitaire

je   cherche

le   motif

la   source

glacée

d'où

j'aurais

jailli

to find

the door   you   need

to   knock

a

with

gentle

barbarism

the   mountain   will

let

you

in

pour　　　**trouver**

la　**porte**

on　a　besoin

d'une　volonté

de

frapper

avec

une　　　　barbarie

douce

la　montagne

vous　fera

entrer

des herbes

ont

toutes ces **fo**rmes

du désir

envie

d'un autre jardin

de prendre

au de**l**à

de **l**a barrière

racine

entre

les   pierres

sèch**es**

wild

all these forms

of

desire

for another

garden

to take

beyond

the barred gates

root

between

dry

stone

walls

excised

by

the white flame

she

smoked

sank

into

her book

offering

for

heat

only the

expiring

gesture

à côté de

la flamme blanche

elle

s'en**lisait**

son livre

n'offrant de sa chaleur

que

le geste

fumait

expirant

échapper

des menus

propos

le vent

s'élance vers

la porte

du village

l'enfant

s'arrache de

la prise

la langue **maternelle**

son hurlement

s'**exprime**

toute

sauvage

escaping

small   talk

                                                wind

                                                                        screams

                                                through

                the

                                child

                                                                wrenches

                                                        free

                                                from

        her

    mother   all   meaning

                                        tongue

                                                unbound

every

being

star

constitutes

dust

a   probe

employed

we

mean

to

sh**in**e

a   new

direction

Acknowledgments

Deep thanks to the sources running through these poems: Ralph Angel, Roland Barthes, Bread & Puppet Theater, René Char, Johann Wolfgang von Goethe, Blind Willie Johnson, Anselm Kiefer, Gabriella Klein, Federico García Lorca, Laurie Sheck, Henry David Thoreau, Jean Valentine, Jessica Washburn.

And deepest thanks to my readers: Jen Bervin, Elizabeth Deshays, David Hinton, Kate Linton.

And to the Dora Maar House for the gifts of time and place.

And to the following journals where these poems appear:

Harvard Review: the poor hide what they can

Leaping Clear: that mare sometimes appeared; now silent becomes listen; what kind of quest is this; I like having nothing

Plant-Human Quarterly: guest bed; wild grasses; des herbes folles

Poetry International: space is not matter; look back at me my love belong here; in my sickness the sky kept spinning; thank you for your very beautiful cross-outs

Volt: lost in lit screens the readers with their books

Washington Square Review: the mother tongue licked me into being

is art the idling silence   is for Ralph Angel and Jean Valentine

The New World: Infinitesimal Epics, Anthony Carelli

Night Talk and Other Poems, Richard Pevear

The 1002nd Night, Debora Greger

Operation Memory, David Lehman

Pass It On, Rachel Hadas

Please make me pretty, I don't want to die: Poems, Tawanda Mulalu

Poems, Alvin Feinman

The Power to Change Geography, Diana O'Hehir

Radioactive Starlings: Poems, Myronn Hardy

Rain in Plural: Poems, Fiona Sze-Lorrain

Reservations: Poems, James Richardson

Returning Your Call: Poems, Leonard Nathan

The River Twice: Poems, Kathleen Graber

River Writing: An Eno Journal, James Applewhite

The Ruined Elegance: Poems, Fiona Sze-Lorrain

Sadness and Happiness: Poems, Robert Pinsky

Scaffolding: Poems, Eléna Rivera

Selected Poems, Jay Wright

Shores and Headlands, Emily Grosholz

Signs and Wonders: Poems, Carl Dennis

Stet: Poems, Dora Malech

Syllabus of Errors: Poems, Troy Jollimore

The Tradition, Albert F. Moritz

The Two Yvonnes: Poems, Jessica Greenbaum

The Unstill Ones: Poems, Miller Oberman

Visiting Rites, Phyllis Janowitz

Walking Four Ways in the Wind, John Allman

Wall to Wall Speaks, David Mus

A Wandering Island, Karl Kirchwey

The Way Down, John Burt

Whinny Moor Crossing, Judith Moffett

A Woman Under the Surface: Poems and Prose Poems, Alicia Ostriker

Yellow Stars and Ice, Susan Stewart